DEBI NIXON

THE ART OF
HOSPITALITY

COMPANION BOOK

A Practical Guide for a

Ministry of Radical Welcome

ABINGDON PRESS | NASHVILLE

THE ART OF HOSPITALITY COMPANION BOOK
REVISED EDITION

A PRACTICAL GUIDE FOR A MINISTRY
OF RADICAL WELCOME

Library of Congress Control Number: 2024936143
ISBN 13: 978-1-7910-3319-4

MANUFACTURED IN THE UNITED STATES OF AMERICA

CONTENTS

Also Available:

The Art of Hospitality
978-1-7910-3320-0 Print
978-1-7910-3321-7 eBook

More Books by Yvonne Gentile

The Greeter and Usher Handbook
Serving from the Heart (with Carol Cartmill)
Leadership from the Heart (with Carol Cartmill)

More Books by Debi Nixon

Catch (with Adam Hamilton)

1

BIBLICAL HOSPITALITY

Every church—and every Christian—is called to practice hospitality. This call is rooted in scripture, where in both the Old and the New Testaments we discover God's desire to use us as conduits of his love to others. When a community of believers truly shares biblical hospitality, loving and welcoming others as God does, it gives people a taste of the kingdom of God.

Biblical hospitality is centered on love of others and particularly love of the stranger. It is focused on servanthood. It demands something from us, and requires that we see things from the perspective of someone else. Biblical hospitality means we are willing to be uncomfortable, taking on the position of a servant so that others can become more comfortable and feel welcome around us. This kind of hospitality surprises the persons who experience it and invites them to take the first or next step in their journey of faith because they begin to feel like they belong.

Examples of hospitality are found throughout the Bible. In the Old Testament we see Abraham welcoming strangers who came to him, offering them water, food, and a place to stop and rest (Genesis 18:2-8).

In Leviticus 19:33-34, God commands the Israelites to show hospitality to strangers or outsiders in their midst, treating them as one of their own—to love them as they love themselves.

This ideal of hospitality continues in the New Testament, where several writers remind us to extend hospitality by opening our homes to others. In Romans 12:13, Paul writes, "Contribute to the needs of God's people, and welcome strangers into your home." The author of 1 Peter similarly encourages his audience, reminding them of the importance of our attitude: "Open your homes to each other without complaining" (1 Peter 4:9). And the writer of Hebrews indicates that showing hospitality could have far-reaching implications: "Don't neglect to open up your homes to guests, because by doing this some have been hosts to angels without knowing it" (Hebrews 13:2). This is exactly what Abraham and Sarah experienced in Genesis 18, when the strangers Abraham welcomed turned out to be God's messengers. Lot (Genesis 19), Gideon (Judges 6), and Manoah (Judges 13) all entertained strangers who turned out to be special messengers from God. Their stories serve as reminders that the people we welcome this week in worship might be people God is working through in our midst.

These New Testament writers recognized the importance of hospitality through Jesus's teaching and example. Through his actions and his words, Jesus showed us what true hospitality—true love for others—looks like and how important it is. When someone asked him what the greatest commandment was, Jesus pointed to love. "He replied, '*You must love the Lord your God with all your heart, with all your being*, and with all your mind. This is the first and greatest commandment. And the second is like it: *You must love your neighbor as you love yourself*'" (Matthew 22:37-39).

Jesus commanded his followers to love one another, even their enemies, and he demonstrated this love by eating with sinners, healing those who hurt, and visiting those who were outcast. Jesus modeled hospitality when he washed his disciples' feet (John 13:12-17), and then he commanded them to do likewise. Jesus invites us into this story of hospitality. When we show hospitality, we are following Jesus's example and obeying his commandments.

Jesus said that when we love one another, the world will know we are his disciples. Love one another. This ethic of love is the defining attribute of the Christian life and it is the heart from which biblical hospitality flows.

Seeing with Fresh Eyes

As individuals and as church communities, we are called to practice hospitality as an outgrowth of the love of Christ. As church communities we recognize the value of hospitality, but the truth is that we don't show hospitality nearly as well as we could. Often strangers find it hard to find a place within our church home. We have unintentionally built barriers that make it difficult for those on the outside to find their way in, and far too often we have become blind to those barriers. Recognizing these barriers requires us to have fresh eyes, to do the hard work of looking through the lens of a first-time guest.

When my parents moved to a new state, they described their difficulty getting into a church. I found that hard to believe; my parents were church regulars who knew what to expect. If anyone could become part of a church community, it was them! During one of my visits, I suggested we attend one of the local churches in their area. I wanted so see if I could help them get connected.

When we arrived, the first service was letting out, and congregants were exiting the building while others were going in. There was no signage directing us to the sanctuary, and there were no greeters to ask for directions. We followed the flow of people going inside, only to discover we were following those going to Sunday school. To get to the sanctuary, we had to go back outside and reenter through another door on the opposite side of the building from where we had parked. Once inside the worship space, we found our way to a seat. Congregants moved around exchanging pleasantries with one another as they waited for the service to begin, but no one spoke to us. We found the worship service difficult to follow because no directions were provided. We didn't know when to stand or sit down. We didn't know the words to several of the liturgies and choruses used in the service. When the service was over, the pastor was at the door greeting his congregation as they were leaving. I was hopeful he would take notice of my parents as we exited, acknowledging their presence and inviting them back. But there was no contact. We felt invisible and out of place. I left feeling sad, knowing that my parents would not return.

My parents are people familiar with church and the Christian life, and they still could not penetrate the barriers of this church. Not only was I sad for them but I was also heartbroken as I envisioned other people—unchurched people—who might have given this church a try and faced the same barriers.

The people in that church probably thought they were friendly and welcoming. And they did appear very friendly with one another. Yet they were so familiar with their community and their space that they didn't see the barriers that prevented guests from getting connected.

Biblical hospitality requires us to remove barriers, especially those we don't notice, so all feel welcomed and experience the love of God within our church home. It begins with a heart to reach people for Christ and an attitude that understands this may mean sacrifice on our part. It means we have to give up things that make us more comfortable. We may have to give up our favorite parking spot so that a guest can park closer to the building. We may have to accept a change in the style of worship to attract a new generation. We may have to step away from the comfort of visiting with our friends to welcome a stranger, a guest.

We sometimes forget what it feels like for a guest to walk through the doors of our church for the first time. They are likely feeling a little uncertain, sensitive to judgment, concerned about being singled out, or feeling uncomfortable because they don't know what to expect. If they have small children to get ready for church, they are also likely stressed before they even leave their driveway. They come with needs, fears, hopes, and expectations. They have a narrative in their mind of what they anticipate their experience will be like.

You have likely heard the adage, "You only have one chance to make a first impression." That's true. And what's more, it often takes only about thirty seconds to form a first impression, and there is research that has shown most will decide within the first seven minutes of their arrival whether they intend to return to your church or not.[1] Thirty seconds to form a first impression. Seven minutes to decide whether or not they'll come back. That's before a worship song has been sung, a prayer has been said, or the pastor has spoken a word of the sermon. Removing barriers has to start from the very first moment a guest walks through your doors.

Some of us may remember our first visit to the church. For others, we have been a part of the church for so long, we may not remember how it felt to be a stranger. But it is likely that each of us has had an experience of being in a setting where we did not know anyone or in a place or situation that was new to us. And we remember the role hospitality, when done well, played in helping us feel comfortable, at ease, accepted, and open to taking another step.

Let's envision the first thirty seconds a guest will experience at your church. Imagine a person coming to your church for the first time. Maybe it's a single mom who is trying to make ends meet; a recent college graduate who has moved to your area to teach in the local elementary school; a fifty-year-old businessman who recently lost his job; a woman who has just found out she has cancer; a young family with a newborn baby thinking they should be in church now that they have a child; a non-English-speaking family who has stumbled upon your church. Whatever their background, consider these things that guests routinely notice and factor into their impression of your church:

- How easy was your website to navigate?
- Can they find your location? Do they know what time worship starts?
- Is parking a challenge?
- Are the grounds well-tended? Is the building clean and well-maintained? Is there clutter in the entry and gathering areas?
- Is there signage to help them easily navigate? Can they find the way to where they need to go?
- Is there a greeter to open doors and welcome them with a smile? Are their children acknowledged?
- Is there a clearly designated place to ask questions and get helpful answers?

- Does anyone sitting near them extend a welcome, or do they feel invisible, left out of the tight groups that already exist?
- Can they follow the flow of worship and participate? Or, does insider language confuse them and leave them sidelined, watching everyone else engage in worship?

With all this in mind, set a timer for thirty seconds. Close your eyes and reflect on the experience of the person you have selected. How are they feeling as they arrive to your church? What is their first thirty seconds like? When the timer is up, continue thinking through their experience. What is their experience of your website like? What do they find as they park, enter the building, then go into the sanctuary? What do they find in the children's area? What people do they encounter at each of these places, and how do these people interact with them? What is their first impression?

You never know what needs people arrive to the church with each weekend. For first-time guests, something compelled them to come. For some it may be the last effort to save a marriage. For others it may be a need for a message of hope after receiving a cancer diagnosis or experiencing a loss. Some may be new to the area, lonely, and looking for friendship. Others may simply be curious about this man named Jesus and have come to see if he is who others say he is. And some are there because a spouse, a mother, or a grandmother dragged them there.

What will they experience at your church?

Giving the Utmost

Taking the time to see your church and its people through the eyes of first-time guests is an important exercise. It can help you to see the barriers, the obstacles for newcomers that you may have stopped noticing long ago. Biblical hospitality means not just recognizing these barriers but also taking the steps to remove them even if that makes us uncomfortable. Welcoming others is central to our mission as followers of Jesus, and it requires devoting everything we have to the cause.

Radical hospitality is what author Robert Schnase describes as that place where Christians offer "the absolute utmost of themselves, their creativity, their abilities, and their energy" to welcome others into the faith. He also says, it is a "spiritual initiative, the practice of an active and genuine love, a graciousness *unaffected by self-interest*" (emphasis added) so that we may receive others.[2]

Hospitality requires that we set aside our self-interest and give the utmost of ourselves to welcome others. When we do this, we are following Jesus by doing the things he did. Consider Jesus's teaching in Matthew 20:26-28: "Whoever wants to be great among you will be your servant. Whoever wants to be first among you will be your slave—just as the Human One didn't come to be served but rather to serve and to give his life to liberate many people." And in Philippians 2:3-5, Paul captures it this way: "Don't do anything for selfish purposes, but with humility think of others as better than yourselves. Instead of each person watching out for their own good, watch out for what is better for others. Adopt the attitude that was in Christ Jesus." You can tell a person whose heart and thinking have been changed. They imitate Jesus. They are willing to welcome and serve others selflessly, sacrificially. They are willing to give up their own comfort so that others can be comfortable.

Yet too often in our churches, we are unwilling to change. We want to invite others into what we are already doing for ourselves, staying within our own comfort zone, meeting our own needs. Instead of asking, *What can we as the church do so that others will be comfortable?* we demand, *What is the church doing so that I am comfortable?* We want the church to serve us, meet our needs, match our preferences.

Yet Christ calls us to a better way, saying that others will know we are Christians by our love. The way we love and care for one another in the church is a reflection of our love for God, but is also an example of God's love to those outside the church. People will be drawn to a church community that treats one another with kindness, respect, and humility and extends this radical welcome to all. When our hearts have been changed by the love of Christ, we can't help ourselves but to share that love with others. Our willingness to put aside our self-interest and put the needs and comforts of others first won't go unnoticed.

I remember an encounter I had with a woman who was a longtime, committed member in our congregation who had been attending the 9 a.m. traditional worship service for years. This was her worship service. This was the time she went to church, and she loved the traditional music. In an attempt to reach younger families in our community, we discovered they had a preference to attend worship at the 9 a.m. hour but were not drawn to the traditional music. So, a decision was made to change the worship style at the 9 a.m. service from traditional to modern. For some church members, this change was too hard to accept. While they were willing to welcome young families into "their service," they did not want anything else to change. Yet, this woman said to me, "While I don't think I am going to like the music, I will love the people it reaches, so I am willing to accept the change." She demonstrated the sacrificial, selfless heart we must have to extend biblical hospitality. She inspired me, and her witness of sacrifice is not something I will ever forget. I love seeing her joy each weekend in "her service" surrounded by the young families it is reaching. And yes, this service did end up reaching many young families—it is now our largest hour for families with children across all our locations.

Biblical hospitality goes beyond friendliness and a willingness to welcome others into what we are already doing. It requires an element of sacrifice. It requires us to move beyond our own comfort to share life with others, even strangers, as we encounter Christ together.

It Starts with You

Biblical hospitality must be a personal value and a church value. Your core values are the guiding principles that support your purpose and vision, shape your culture, reflect what is important, and influence your behavior. Within the church, biblical hospitality is not the sole responsibility of a ministry team called the hospitality team. It's not just the job of the greeters, ushers, and pastor. Biblical hospitality is the way ministry is done by each person who calls your church home. It starts with you.

Biblical hospitality has been a value at Resurrection, where I serve, from the beginning. It defines who we are as a church and how we approach ministry, and it has been modeled by Adam Hamilton, our senior pastor. By his actions he has modeled how to extend hospitality and welcome people. He made it a priority and said, "This is the kind of church we are going to be."

With a marriage under stress, demanding careers, a one-year-old, and a three-year-old, my husband and I decided we would give church a try. Maybe it could help us. We arrived for our first visit to Church of the

Resurrection hesitant and anxious. And let's be honest: we were likely running late, one of our children was probably crying, and we undoubtedly had a spat on the way there. I don't remember exactly, but I suspect each of these is probable. These are the conditions under which many arrive each week.

Under these already strained conditions, we wondered if we would know where to go and what to do when we arrived. Would anyone speak to us? Would our children be OK in this unfamiliar place? And as if that were not enough to create anxiety for our first visit, did I mention that the church was meeting in a funeral home?! I can honestly say we were not "dying" to go in that day. (Bad joke, I know.)

When we arrived, there was a young man in the parking lot greeting people as they arrived. When we got out of our car, he recognized immediately that we were new, so he came and personally escorted us into the church. He made certain that our children were checked into the nursery and introduced us to an usher who helped us find a seat. When worship started, it was engaging. It was then that I recognized that the young man who had greeted us in the parking lot was the pastor.

That encounter was over thirty years ago. Our lives were changed by the welcome we received, our marriage saved, and our faith was nurtured as we have been discipled. We were transformed by the experience of hospitality that welcomed two strangers.

It is the responsibility of the leadership to cast the vision, set the example, and call the congregation members to move beyond their comfort zones to extend hospitality. At my church, our pastor modeled hospitality from the beginning and continues to set the example today. It is a strong, nonnegotiable value where thousands more have followed his example. But it can't be only the senior pastor or the hospitality team. It starts with each member personally accepting responsibility for extending welcome. Leaders, volunteers, and members in all parts of the church are critical in safeguarding and championing a strong hospitality value. It starts with each of us. It starts with me. It starts with you.

No matter what role you have at your church— whether out front leading worship or behind the scenes; clergy, paid staff, or volunteer; worship leader or nursery volunteer; usher or the person who happens to sit next to someone new—you are the physical representation of Christ to others.

So biblical hospitality is modeled by you. You model the desired behaviors, energize the hospitality movement, and reinforce this value within your church. Your visible commitment sets the tone for others to follow.

This mindset, this acceptance of personal responsibility, forces us to consider how we are faithfully representing Christ to our community and our world. If forces us to live out the hospitality that Jesus modeled for us with every step of his feet, every encounter he had with others, every word he spoke, every healing hand he placed on someone who was in need. And your representation doesn't stop when you leave the church.

You carry that same representation to the restaurant, the grocery store, your child's or grandchild's soccer game, your workplace, your neighborhood, and your family. In a world that can be full of division, you model something different.

The hospitality you demonstrate is a conduit to help people encounter Christ.

Let's remember that biblical hospitality is more than just being friendly or nice to people. It is more than doing things out of obligation. It is more than bending over backwards to meet the needs of others at the expense of your own comfort. It's more than a hello at the door, organized bulletins, well-designed programs, beautiful landscaping, and smiles. Biblical hospitality is the way you engage and interact with others that helps bring them into the transforming presence of the body of Christ that is the church. Biblical hospitality forces us to move beyond our own comfort to seek out the stranger around us, both inside the church and outside the church in the community. And it starts with you.

How to Show Excellent Hospitality

Hospitality has everything to do with how we make people feel. Did we help them feel comfortable—physically, emotionally, and spiritually? Does the appearance of the facility, helpful signage, the welcome of a congregation who had anticipated their presence, and an experience of God's grace through worship make them feel at home and invited, encouraged to take a next step?

Churches with leaders and congregants who practice radical hospitality offer a surprising and unexpected quality of depth and authenticity in their care for others and desire to help others feel more comfortable. Strangers or guests to churches who demonstrate this level of hospitality sense: (1) These people really care about me; (2) They really want the best for me; (3) I am not a number or an outsider at this church; (4) I am being invited into the body of Christ with them.

So, let's examine a few practical ideas to extend hospitality. These are ways to move beyond friendliness and doing what is perfunctory, and instead to prioritize surprising our guests and strangers among us, inviting them into the presence of Christ.

Here are a few ideas:

- Park in the farthest spaces when you arrive to church, saving the closest parking spaces for guests. It is something you can also practice when out at the grocery store, work, or community events. It becomes a discipline, teaching you to think of others' needs before your own.

- Wear your church name tag. If your church does not have name tags, this may be a practice to start. Name tags immediately help to break down barriers so we can call one another by name and help guests do the same.

- Give up your favorite seat in worship and sit in the middle of the row and toward the front, leaving the back rows available and the end seats open for guests so they do not have to step over you to get to a seat.

- Greet guests in a friendly manner, without asking directly if they are new. Simply extend welcome and introduce yourself by saying something like, "Hello, I am so glad you are here, my name is…"

- Avoid over greeting. Guests want to be acknowledged but not singled out as new, and they don't want to be overwhelmed by too many greetings.

- When giving directions, walk with the person to the location instead of pointing. Say, "Let me show you."

- If you have coffee available, pour two cups of coffee. Give the first to the person waiting in line behind you and enjoy the second one yourself. You will likely engage in a great conversation with the person you just handed the coffee to, but even if not it's a kind action that surprises and delights the other person.

- Be a connector, introducing guests to others. If you are greeting a guest when a friend approaches, say, "James, I want you to meet Bob."
- Always consider how your actions, behaviors, and decisions impact the ability for a guest to be comfortable. It will take sacrifice and extra work on your part, but it is worth it.
- At our church, we encourage our congregation to keep two rules in mind, which helps them be attentive to guests without being overbearing.
  ◊ **The 3-minute rule:** Spend three minutes before and after the worship service or ministry program greeting those you do not know. So often people visit with those they know at church and believe they have a friendly congregation. Yet when guests arrive, their experience too often is that, other than ushers and greeters, no one else speaks to them. Or when they leave, they don't receive the same greeting as when they arrived because

the congregants have migrated to conversations with those they know. The "3-minute rule" reminds us to be intentional about greeting and getting to know someone we don't know at the beginning and at the end. This is a practice you can also use at work, a community event, a family gathering, or anywhere else you encounter new people. We tend to gravitate toward those we feel most comfortable with, and by stretching ourselves in all our environments, we can make hospitality a natural practice. It may never be comfortable, but it will become a way we live as those who love Christ.

◊ **The 10-foot rule:** You are responsible for the environment ten feet around you. Greet and introduce yourself to those within ten feet of you. No one wants the entire congregation converging on them when they visit. Instead, those who are closest take responsibility for engaging each person within ten feet of them. And this

applies to facility needs within ten feet
of you too. If you see something in the
environment that needs attention—
papers on the floor, a spill—take
responsibility to address it.

The ministry of hospitality is not about growing the church. While growth will be the outcome, we do not start with this in mind. I love a quote attributed to Mother Teresa: "Never worry about numbers. Help one person at a time and always start with the person nearest you."

Let us not forget the message at the heart of all we do: God loves us and sent his only son to save us. Jesus is the answer to the deepest needs of our heart, and the church is the place where Jesus calls his followers to carry out his ministry. You are the physical representation of Christ. When we believe this, we can't help ourselves! Our only response is to extend the same hospitality we have received through Christ to others. The gift of hospitality you extend to others literally changes lives!

Our ministry of hospitality must be more than an initial encounter. It must be a value, the nonnegotiable practice we demonstrate so that new people can enter the Christian community, encounter Christ, be discipled, and then go back out to be representatives of this same hospitality.

By showing we are anticipating and ready for guests, and that they are welcomed and accepted, we become the physical manifestation of Christ's love and welcome for those who come. When we make their experience exceptionally positive, their preconceived notions about church (and Christians) are deconstructed. They are open to returning, which is the first step in a life of faith.

Your role at the church, whether behind-the-scenes or public-facing, is critical to people experiencing a taste of God's kingdom here on earth. Before anyone decides to grow deeper in their faith, be healed in their brokenness, or get connected in the community, they have to feel they are welcomed and accepted. As a congregant in your church, the hospitality you share is connected to what your guests experience and whether they ultimately return.

Time to Get Uncomfortable

Let's be honest once more: it is more comfortable and easier to share hospitality with those we already know. And the art of hospitality may come more easily for some than for others. Some naturally have the spiritual gift of hospitality, while others must work at it a bit harder. The bottom line, though, is that God uses people like you and me to be his messengers of the good news of Christ. When we practice hospitality, we are used by God to be a part of his kingdom work in changing lives and transforming the world.

With intentionality, commitment, accountability, and prayer, we can transform our churches into places that extend unconditional welcome for all. But it starts with the transformation of your heart and mine, so that we recognize the unmerited gift we have received in Christ who welcomed us.

The table at the Last Supper where Jesus modeled one of his acts of hospitality was filled with imperfect people. James and John wanted the best seats; Peter was bold and likely a bit too aggressive; Thomas was a pessimist and doubter; Matthew had been a tax collector; and Judas ultimately betrayed Jesus and his friends. While this is a look at just half of those present, you might be able to identify a few of these imperfect people within your own congregation. You are likely one. Yet all but one of these imperfect leaders went on to be used by Christ for the transformation of the world.

The God of the universe, through Jesus, invites you to the table. He has called you to be his hands and feet, offering hospitality, piercing the darkness with light, so that all are welcomed in his house. And by these acts of hospitality, others will know we are his disciples.

Let us pray: *Jesus, I give my life to you in response to the gift of love and grace you have given to me. I admit that at times I am too comfortable and unwilling to change. What is required is scary. But today I say yes to becoming uncomfortable, accepting your command to love the stranger and welcome the stranger into the church home. Help me find ways to be your hands and feet, to begin practicing hospitality in all aspects of my life, so that it flows naturally in all that I do, bearing witness to my love for you. Amen.*

27

Personal Reflection

1. When you read the word *hospitality*, what images first come to mind?

2. Can you remember a time when you received hospitality that surprised you, good or bad? How did you feel? Share your experience with another.

3. Why is change hard for most of us to accept? What changes are hard for you to accept? Why?

4. Why do you think the first thirty seconds are so important to a first-time guest?

5. What do guests experience within the first thirty seconds or first few minutes at your church? What changes need to be made to enhance their physical, emotional, and spiritual experience?

6. Review the list of simple steps you might take to extend hospitality. What will be the most challenging for you? Why?

7. What did you think of the 3-minute and 10-foot rule? How could these two simple rules become actionable at your church?

8. What is one action of hospitality you will commit to pursuing?

2

THE MINISTRY OF NOTICE

My grandmother had a stroke toward the end of her life. During a visit, I took her to McDonald's to enjoy a vanilla shake. While there, she observed me speaking with strangers while waiting in line, thanking the employees, and helping clean a table for a family whose hands were full. When we were alone, I was surprised by the question she asked, "Why are you so nice to everyone?" I responded, "Because I had a grandmother who taught me about the love of Jesus, who commands us to love everyone. I am doing what my grandmother taught me." The corner of her lips turned up into a sly grin; she remembered

Jesus's love despite the stroke that had taken some of her mental abilities, and she was making certain I remembered too.

Hospitality arises from a deep, relentless love. Because of the love we receive from Christ, we find that when we love him in return we can't help ourselves and must share his love with others, including strangers.

The most fundamental expression of love is attention. It's noticing. When we notice others around us, whether they are a child, a spouse, a friend, a coworker, or a stranger, it says, "I see you. You matter." When we notice something that needs to be addressed, and we act on it, it matters. When my husband notices that the trash needs to be emptied and does it, I feel like the most loved woman on the planet. There is tremendous power in just noticing.

Churches that practice biblical hospitality NOTICE. They notice the stranger, they notice the person in need, they notice when something needs attention. These churches know that there is no hospitality until we first notice. Have you ever been somewhere where people walked by you without making any kind of eye contact or acknowledging your presence? Maybe this was even at church? Church, we must do better.

We are called to be in fellowship with one another, but this can't happen if we aren't even noticing people.

Being Present in the Moment

To notice we must be aware of our surroundings, both the physical space and the people around us, and be present in the moment. Each week we have guests who cross our path. If we are to practice hospitality, it is our calling to notice strangers, greet them eagerly, and care for their needs.

However, too often we are distracted—even in church. We can get so busy doing the work of the church that the tasks required compete for our ability to notice others. During one of our annual leadership conferences, we ran low on sandwiches. As I was running through a door with a cart full of additional sandwiches, a guest noticed that I needed help. He opened the door and was preparing to offer a word of greeting, but without looking at him I ran through the door. Several weeks later I received a kind but forthright letter. You see, he had heard me speak on the power of hospitality at a conference a few months earlier and had decided to make a visit to see it in action. He helped me see that my actions that day did not match my teaching at the conference. I had been distracted by what I was doing, so distracted by the task at hand that I didn't take one second, just one second, to look up and see a stranger standing there. Eye contact and a brief "thank you" would have said, "I see you. What you have done matters. Thank you." I needed to be less rushed and more present in the moment.

Rushing often keeps us from being able to notice. When we are rushing, like I was to deliver the sandwiches, it is hard to pay attention to anything other than our immediate task.

It's important to reflect on times we prioritize the task instead of prioritizing the ministry of notice. It happens easily. We are busy restocking the brochures at the information booth and miss seeing the person who needs help. Maybe we arrive to the church where no one is greeting at the door or passing out bulletins, but we don't step in because this is not our scheduled weekend to serve. Maybe we're checking our phones or running through our to-do list for the afternoon and don't see the guest who is standing alone in our sanctuary, wondering why they even bothered coming.

In our fast-paced world, we have dozens of distractions that compete for our attention. Technology has created ways for us to be more connected than ever before, but it has also diminished our ability to notice and be fully present to those near us in an undistracted way. Have you ever been with someone who is not fully present with you? They are looking at their phone, looking past you, fidgeting. When we are not fully present, others notice. This lack of attention creates barriers that are hard to overcome. In this world, our willingness to connect with those around us, to notice them and acknowledge them, can go a long way toward helping them feel seen and welcomed.

Biblical hospitality modeled by Jesus requires us to *give others an unhurried moment*. That's why we ask our volunteers to arrive early to get their assignments, needed supplies, and instructions. We want them not to be distracted or rushed, but fully present in the moment, ready and prepared to notice. To give others an unhurried moment, we must press pause on what we are doing and give our complete attention and focus to the person in front of us. And that's something you can do not just at church, but as a part of your daily life. Notice the people around you, give the person in front of you the gift of an unhurried moment, and watch what a difference it makes.

Recently, I watched as my daughter approached the door of a building. She was pushing a stroller with her two-year-old, had her newborn baby in a snuggle sack around her chest, and was balancing an item on the top of the stroller. There was another person entering the door immediately ahead of her. The person was so distracted that, even after exchanging pleasantries with my daughter, she didn't pause from what she was doing to hold the door open for her. This person went in, letting the door close because she was so preoccupied with her own tasks.

Contrast that with undistracted volunteers who notice guests approaching and eagerly serve by opening doors, providing welcome, and assisting them with any needs. I love seeing the response of the guests who are surprised and blessed by the gesture.

A favorite remembrance is what I observed one Easter. Like most churches, we had many guests arriving for the first time, and on this particular Easter it was raining. Actually, let me be more specific: it was pouring. Yet, before our guests could even get out of their cars, our volunteers were there with umbrellas helping them into the building. They sprang into action, grabbing umbrellas from inside the church and even from their own cars, and they eagerly approached guests. They noticed the rain, noticed the guests, and noticed they had an opportunity to help. The ministry of notice requires us to be present in the moment, to recognize a person or a need, and then to accept the responsibility to act.

When We Notice, We Follow the Example of Jesus

Jesus was busy, yet scripture is full of stories of his willingness to be interrupted when he noticed others in need. Through his life and ministry, he has given us a powerful example of love and welcome, which we see in the way he noticed and responded to those who crossed his path in need.

Jesus Noticed Those in Need of Healing

In Luke 8, we read of a woman who had been bleeding for twelve years. She had spent her entire livelihood on doctors, to no avail. Jesus and his disciples were surrounded by overwhelming crowds pressing in on them, *smothering crowds* as the Common English Bible puts it. And Jesus was busy, on his way to heal another person, a young girl who was dying. Yet when this woman touched the hem of Jesus's garment, she was instantly healed. Jesus noticed. He stopped what he was doing to be present with her.

As Jesus moved forward, he faced smothering crowds.

A woman was there who had been bleeding for twelve years. She had spent her entire livelihood on doctors, but no one could heal her. She came up behind him and touched the hem of his clothes, and at once her bleeding stopped.

"Who touched me?" Jesus asked.

When everyone denied it, Peter said, "Master, the crowds are surrounding you and pressing in on you!"

But Jesus said, "Someone touched me. I know that power has gone out from me."

When the woman saw that she couldn't escape notice, she came trembling and fell before Jesus. In front of everyone, she explained why she had touched him and how she had been immediately healed.

"Daughter, your faith has healed you," Jesus said. "Go in peace."

(vv. 42-48)

In 2009 near the Sea of Galilee, construction workers uncovered a first-century synagogue believed to be one where Jesus taught. It was also discovered that this was the ancient town from where Mary of Magdala had come. Today there is a chapel built on this site honoring women in the Bible. Inside, there is a magnificent mural depicting the story of the woman who touched the hem of Jesus's garment. You can read about it and see a photo by visiting www.old.magdala.org/duc-in-altum/and clicking on the "Encounter Chapel" button. When you walk into the room where it is located, it takes your breath away. I have had the privilege of seeing it a few times, and each time I am overwhelmed at the power of seeing the hand of the woman reaching through the crowds to touch his hem.

When I stand before this mural, I am amazed at the ability of Jesus to be fully present, even in the midst of all he had to accomplish, all that was expected of him, and all the distractions that he surely encountered. Jesus noticed the woman who touched him, and it transformed her life. When we practice the ministry of notice, as Jesus did, it changes lives.

There may be times when the Holy Spirit will prompt you to pause in the middle of what you are doing to take notice of something or someone around you. These are divine moments. Jeff, one of our pastors, is highly attuned to the nudging of the Holy Spirit. He notices body language and has a great intuition, so he's more aware than most of when someone is in need, has a question, or simply would like to connect. He has been an incredible mentor to me, and has encouraged me to slow down, pay attention, and be aware of when God wants to use me in ministry with another person. But it requires a slowing and willingness to be fully present even when we have other things to do.

Several months ago, I was running out of my office to attend a meeting. As I was walking down the hallway, I passed our Memorial Garden where loved ones are inurned. As I looked outside, I noticed a woman sitting on a bench hunched over with her face in her hands. If I stopped to see if there was anything I could do, I would be late for my meeting, so my first thought was to keep going. But Jeff has taught me to be attentive to noticing others, so I stopped and went outside. As I approached her, I could tell she had been crying. I introduced myself, and told her that I simply wanted to let her know she was loved and asked if there was anything I could do for her. We talked for several minutes as she shared her story of being estranged from a member of her family. She had come to the Memorial Garden where her dad was inurned with hopes of experiencing peace and reconciliation. Before leaving I took her hands in mine, prayed for her, and reminded her of the unconditional love of her heavenly father. Later that day I received an email from her in which she said, "I was sitting there feeling alone. You saw me and it made my whole day. I think God wanted you to be walking by at that exact time today. Thank you for stopping."

Do you ever experience a nudging that tells you to do something? Maybe you have said, "I was in the right place at the right time." To practice the ministry of notice, we must be attentive to these promptings by the Holy Spirit.

Jesus paid attention to the nudge. He stopped and noticed the woman who touched the hem of his robe, and she was healed. This is the power of the ministry of notice we are each called to. Each day we walk past others as we go from Point A to Point B. We are surrounded by faces of individuals whose paths just happen to intersect with ours for a few seconds. Will we notice them? Will we be open to what God might be willing to do through our interaction with them?

Jesus Noticed Those Whom Others Passed By

While going to a festival, Jesus passed the pool of Bethsaida, a gathering place for people hoping to be healed. He noticed a paralyzed man who had been near the pool for thirty-eight years. While others kept going, Jesus stopped, spoke with him, heard his story, and healed him.

> When Jesus saw him lying there, knowing that he had already been there a long time, he asked him, "Do you want to get well?"
>
> The sick man answered him, "Sir, I don't have anyone who can put me in the water when it is stirred up. When I'm trying to get to it, someone else has gotten in ahead of me."
>
> Jesus said to him, "Get up! Pick up your mat and walk." Immediately the man was well, and he picked up his mat and walked.
>
> (John 5:6-9)

How often do we pass by common places where people gather and just keep going? For thirty-eight years those traveling through Jerusalem would pass by this place, and yet no one stopped to help this man. Too often we get accustomed to seeing something or someone over and over, and we lose a sense of curiosity. They become part of the backdrop, and we don't see opportunities to welcome them or extend God's love to them.

Our ministry of notice requires us to have eyes to see like Jesus. Is there something or someone in your church or community you have passed by for months, maybe years, that is in need of your notice? Maybe something within your facility needs to be addressed. Maybe a guest has slipped into worship a few times, but you haven't taken the time to introduce yourself yet. In your personal life, it could be a coworker who needs you to notice them more. Or it may be the person standing on the street corner you pass each day.

For a year, a car sat unmoved in front of my neighbor's house. One afternoon, a bright orange tag on the antenna caught my attention. Knowing these tags were placed on cars by law enforcement before they were towed away, I decided to contact my neighbor to see if everything was OK. To my surprise, I discovered her husband had passed away unexpectedly the year before. A year! I missed noticing a neighbor in need. The unmoved car became a common sight and I lost a sense of curiosity.

To practice the ministry of notice, we must have open eyes and a willingness to stop. We must be willing to disengage from what we are doing to give our full attention to others. And we must not let tasks distract us from noticing the needs of those around us.

A church in the Northwest began to recognize that each morning, high school students walked in front of their building on their way to school, a normal, everyday occurrence that had gone unnoticed for years. One cold day they set up a table outside the building and began offering hot chocolate and coffee to the students every day as they passed. From this small gesture, relationships with the students developed into new ministries.

They noticed, they got curious, and they acted. When we notice those others pass by, when we begin to notice the everyday things that have stopped catching our attention, it creates opportunities for God to work through us.

Jesus Noticed the Spiritually Needy

Jesus noticed those in need of spiritual care, but he had to look up. In Luke 19 we read of a tree that hundreds of people had walked past. If any of them had tilted their head back a bit to look up into that sycamore tree, they would have seen a man sitting there named Zacchaeus.

He was up in the sycamore tree because he was waiting for Jesus. Zacchaeus was a rich man, a businessman, who had heard about Jesus and hoped to see him. As a tax collector—a chief tax collector at that—Zacchaeus was considered a sinner, an enemy. Others passed by Zacchaeus that day and either didn't notice him at all or saw him and dismissed him. But Jesus noticed and stopped.

> Jesus entered Jericho and was passing through town. A man there named Zacchaeus, a ruler among tax collectors, was rich. He was trying to see who Jesus was, but, being a short man, he couldn't because of the crowd. So he ran ahead and climbed up a sycamore tree so he could see Jesus, who was about to pass that way. When Jesus came to that spot, he looked up and said, "Zacchaeus, come down at once. I must stay in your home today." So Zacchaeus came down at once, happy to welcome Jesus.
>
> Everyone who saw this grumbled, saying, "He has gone to be the guest of a sinner."
>
> Zacchaeus stopped and said to the Lord, "Look, Lord, I give half of my possessions to the poor. And if I have cheated anyone, I repay them four times as much."
>
> (vv. 1-8)

43

Jesus not only saw Zacchaeus but also stopped what he was doing, called him by name, and offered hospitality, saying, "Let's eat together!" It was radical hospitality. It was surprising. It was life-transforming, as we read in Luke 19:9-10: "Today, salvation has come to this household because he too is a son of Abraham. The Human One came to seek and save the lost."

How many had walked past that tree and did not notice a man sitting there? Or, maybe they did notice him, but judgments and biases against interacting with a man like him kept them from engaging. There are Zacchaeuses in our midst, too, whether in our churches or in our communities. What distracts us from looking up to notice them, to welcome them? What judgments and biases might we have to abandon to welcome everyone?

Jesus Noticed the Children

I recently read a social media post where the writer asked responders to share about times when they had been made to feel unwelcomed in a church. It was overwhelming to read all the responses about churches who had made someone's children feel unwelcomed. Some shared stories of being asked to leave the sanctuary because of their children. Others shared examples of churches not having spaces or ministry prepared for their children. Yet Jesus welcomed children and commands us to do the same.

> People were bringing children to Jesus so that he would bless them. But the disciples scolded them. When Jesus saw this, he grew angry and said to them, "Allow the children to come to me. Don't forbid them, because God's kingdom belongs to people like these children. I assure you that whoever doesn't welcome God's kingdom like a child will never enter it." Then he hugged the children and blessed them.
>
> (Mark 10:13-16)

A couple at our church shared their story of moving to Kansas City and beginning the process of looking for a church home. They had three boys under the age of five. The size of Resurrection concerned them, but when the greeter not only greeted them but also greeted their boys by getting down on one knee to be at their level, that concern was alleviated. Because of this simple gesture, they decided to give the church a second try. On the second visit, when they entered the same greeter not only welcomed them in the same way but remembered the names of their boys. In that moment, Resurrection became their church home. This is the power of the ministry of notice.

We encourage all of our greeters to greet not only adults but also children. Activity books and crayons are visible in the sanctuary so that children know they are welcome in worship. As those who value children, you must find ways to clearly communicate that children are welcomed. And it must start with each person—leaders, volunteers, and congregants— adopting the attitude that children are welcome and should feel at home among you.

When we eagerly pursue hospitality and strive to meet the needs of guests, we become conduits of God's love, grace, healing, care, and presence for them.

There are families in your community eager to find a church home but who want a place that will welcome their children. Do you notice them?

There is a woman in your community seeking to break through the barriers of the crowd, looking for healing, comfort, a word of encouragement. Do you notice her?

There is a man paralyzed by life who needs your help to take a next step. Do you notice him?

There are a spiritually hungry people who look at your community and wonder if they can belong. Do you notice them?

Do you notice the stranger in your midst who wants to break into your circle, to be a part of the community and take a next step in their journey of faith? Do you notice the young mom who simply needs to have a door opened?

Reliable Systems for Noticing

Committing to follow the example of Christ in offering hospitality means we will find ourselves being stretched outside of our comfort zone at times. We must be ready and willing to have our normal routines interrupted to be fully able to notice—to be fully attentive.

One way to help you do this, especially in your church setting, is to establish new routines that will encourage noticing. Developing reliable systems for noticing, recognizing, and responding to others will help your church as a whole be better at a ministry of notice, and participating in these systems or practices will help make noticing more natural for you.

As an example, you must find a way for people to communicate their prayer needs. Some churches do this during a time called "joys and concerns," when the needs of the community are shared in an open setting during worship. While this might work in your setting, when you consider the practice through the lens of a guest, it seems like something that can easily make guests feel uncomfortable. Most won't openly share a concern, and as they listen to concerns of people that others seem to know personally, it reminds them that they are not a part of the inner circle.

At our church, a form for prayer requests is on our website, and prayer request cards are available in our chapels. We encourage each person to complete a prayer request card. The completed cards are prayed over by a team of committed volunteers weekly. These volunteers follow up by sending an email and a handwritten note letting the person know prayer has been offered. Requests that need pastoral attention are given to a pastor and receive a prompt response.

This system lets us recognize the needs of members and guests, and it notices the likely presence of guests and what they might be feeling. We "notice" guests, in other words, by using a system that will be more comfortable for them than a different practice like "joys and concerns."

Another practice is that we must find a way to get people's names—to be aware of guests and have a way of following up with them. Churches do this differently. Some have a location where guests are given a gift for providing their contact information, while others ask guests to fill out and turn in a connect card to an usher.

Some churches ask only their guests to complete a connection card, but we ask our members to sign in also because we know that singling out our guests makes them uncomfortable. Having the members complete the sign-in sets an example for the guests to follow. Prior to COVID-19, we passed a physical notebook down each row to collect this information. Since COVID-19, we have had to deploy processes that have less physical contact so our sign-in is online. As a part of the worship service, intentional time is devoted to providing instructions on how to enter attendance. It is important for members and regular visitors to also sign in each week so that if they miss worship, it is also noticed, and someone can provide timely follow-up with them as well.

Some churches trying to establish this practice encounter resistance from the members. Some members simply do not want to sign in, stating that the church knows they are there. While this statement may or may not be true, we remember we do not always do things for our own benefit. Instead we do them to benefit others. If your church decides to show hospitality to guests by adopting a different practice for prayer requests or signing in (or anything else), it may take some getting used to. Change is never easy, but remember why it's important and participate willingly and eagerly. Even if you are not a leader, set an example for others to follow. Taking attendance and recognizing prayer requests are important practices that help your church notice and care for members and guests. And the change may create new opportunities for you personally to show hospitality to guests you've never had before.

Our church uses volunteers, not just pastors, to pray for and reach out to those who have submitted prayer requests. Volunteering for a ministry like this at your church allows you to practice radical hospitality by praying for the needs of others.

Our follow-up practice for our first-time guests is another way volunteers get involved in showing hospitality. The practice was established by our pastor when our church first started and continues to this day. Every first-time guest receives a coffee mug delivered to their doorstep within forty-eight hours of their visit. When Pastor Adam first started this practice of "mugging," he would go home following the morning worship service, have a quick lunch with his family, and then get back in his car to deliver mugs. He delivered every first-time guest coffee mug for many years and is now joined by hundreds of other volunteers who understand the important witness to hospitality this gesture brings.

Sundays are busy, but our "muggers" know how important their ministry is to increase the likelihood that a first-time guest will return. I have heard countless times from our guests of how surprised they are that we followed up so quickly, and they talk about it. It sends a message to them that they are noticed, and they matter. It's hospitality through the lens of notice.

What can you do at your church to notice and extend hospitality to others, whether that's through an existing volunteer opportunity or through a new practice? How can you model a ministry of notice through your attitude and your actions?

Timely Follow-Up

Timely follow-up is a value at Resurrection, and it is an important extension of the ministry of notice. Noticing must happen first, but noticing is only the first step. It must be continued through action, following through with personal attention that surprises and delights others. Personal follow-up with a nonperishable gift within forty-eight hours to your first-time guests; an email or phone call in response to a question within twenty-four hours; a note expressing thanks or offering words of encouragement or condolences; inviting lapsed members to reconnect signaling that you noticed they were missing; promptly contacting someone who has signed up to serve—these are all a part of a ministry of notice.

We must consider each opportunity we have to interact with someone as an opportunity to be used by God to help them in their faith journey. Your church must have processes in place that help to make certain follow-up happens, and you can play an important role by volunteering, setting an example, and making excellent follow-through a personal commitment of your own.

Earlier I shared my story of coming to Resurrection for the first time and experiencing exceptional hospitality offered by none other than the pastor. Here is another part of my story. My husband and I tried to get connected in a church a few years before we found Resurrection. We signed up for a Sunday school class. No one called us back. We signed up to play on the coed softball team. No one called us back. We signed up for other opportunities, and not one time did anyone follow up. Because we were unnoticed, we easily slipped out the back door. And it would be more than three years before we stepped through the door of a church again.

The ministry of notice requires that follow-up systems are a priority. A defined system helps guard against follow-up that is missed, particularly when requests come into the general voicemail or email account. There should be accountability on everyone's part that if there is a sign-up form, RSVP, ministry question, or some other request, responses are made within twenty-four or forty-eight hours. Jesus left no one behind. We remember in scripture the parables of the one: the one lost sheep, the one lost coin, and the one lost son (Luke 15). The power in these stories is that Jesus cared for the one who is missing. Jesus came to save the lost, so that not one would slip through the cracks. How do we have the eyes of Jesus and notice the same?

While the church should have reliable systems to help ensure no one falls through the cracks—which you should support!—it's also important to remember our individual responsibility in the ministry of notice and follow-through. The 3-minute and 10-foot rules provide guidance helping us remember to offer a warm greeting to each guest we encounter, starting with the person right in front of us. We remember our responsibility to notice when people are alone, look lost, or need assistance. We notice if there is an issue in the environment or facility that needs to be addressed such as trash, a spill on the floor, or countertops in the bathroom that need to be wiped down. And, for the ministries we help lead, we make follow-up a priority. We understand the value of notice and follow-up, and we do something about it.

Changing Lives

The ministry of notice helps to remove barriers. It gets the attention of a guest when they receive hospitality that surprises them, and it gives people a sense that we care. This is what we are called to do as a church. We are God's instruments in bearing light into places of darkness when people are hurting, grieving, and in need. We bear the message of the good news in our welcome of all.

It requires that we truly notice others outside of our own purview and see what's happening around us. And for some, that does not come naturally. We are not as comfortable encountering strangers as others are. This may require us to work a bit harder with a willing spirit, letting ourselves be uncomfortable to help someone else be comfortable.

The ministry of notice is not something we do only within the walls of the church. As we discussed in the last chapter, biblical hospitality extends into every environment in our lives. A smile while you wait in line at the store goes a long way, and research shows that smiling improves our own mood. And our smiles make those around us feel better too.

I have this routine when I am stopped at a stoplight to look at the person in the car next to me and wonder about how their day is going. I then follow up with a quick prayer for them. It's a silly thing I started doing many years ago following the death of my great-grandmother. I was fortunate to grow up with my great-grandparents in my life, not experiencing my first family death until I was in my late twenties. On the day my great-grandmother passed, I was driving to my hometown in southwest Missouri, wanting the world to pause for a moment. I was surprised that everything around me was still going on as normal. "Hey, you in that blue car, why are you laughing and smiling? Don't you know what has happened? Don't you see my tears? Don't you know that my great-grandmother just died?" I felt that everyone should pause for a moment to notice my grief and say "I am so sorry for your loss." So today whenever I stop at a red light, I pause for a moment to wonder and pray for the person next to me. Who knows what they might be going through.

Let's be honest, we struggle at times with being unaware of others' needs. The presence of others around us is such a normal part of life that, unless someone does something unusual that catches our attention, we can be oblivious. We must really work to make ourselves think of all those faces as being anything more than the subject of occasional passing.

We may even need to acknowledge our own biases and judgments to notice others around us. The couple with the child who is making too much noise, the man whose clothes are dirty, the woman with a lot of tattoos, the family whose child has special needs, the woman who does not speak English well, the couple whose skin color is different from ours, or the same-gendered couple—do you welcome them by extending biblical hospitality, or do you hope someone else will do it and find a way to sit as far away as possible?

At one of our locations, a man released from prison and living in a halfway house visited on the first weekend after he was released. The man got up on Sunday morning and left, simply looking to find a church where he could get a bulletin that he could take back to the halfway house. This would be evidence that he had gone to church, fulfilling a condition of his release, but he had no intention of staying for worship. His clothes were dirty, and he was still wearing the orange issued shower shoes on his feet. His plan was just to wander the city streets for a few hours by himself, then return to the halfway house with the bulletin in hand.

Something happened when he arrived at our church that day. While he was expecting to be greeted with unapproving looks, he was instead greeted by someone at the door, who looked him in the eye and offered him a cup of coffee. An usher helped him find a seat, and although he had the required bulletin in his hand, something compelled him to stay for just a few more minutes. The music started, drawing him in. And then it came time for the greeting. In that moment, he experienced human touch for the first time in years, through a simple handshake and word of welcome. He had been noticed. He mattered. He met Christ through acts of hospitality, practiced by ordinary individuals who greeted, gave coffee, and shook hands—all with the love of Jesus.

Sometimes, in order to notice others, we need to let go of biases or judgments. Sometimes we need to let go of the tasks we are preoccupied with. Or we may need to let go of our own desires, or our pride, or anything else that keeps us from loving others as we love ourselves. And in some of our churches, the years of not seeing guests and our own disappointment and acceptance of the status quo might be blinders to our ministry of notice. We've gotten so accustomed to the way things are that we can't imagine anything different, so why try?

God is calling us to a new vision. Our pursuit and practice of the ministry of notice must be a priority as we invite others to discover a God who loves and seeks them, a God who is near and wants to be in relationship with them, a God who is good, a God who heals, and a God who gave his life on our behalf through his son Jesus.

When my daughter was twenty-one, two of her friends decided to attend a Sunday evening worship service at our church. Neither girl had gone to church regularly, participated in youth group, or attended a summer church camp. But for some reason that afternoon, one of the girls said to the other, "Let's go to church tonight." And they did.

When the invitation came for Communion, both decided to share in the meal. When they returned to their seats, one of the young women noticed that her friend had a tear in her eye. Following the service, they picked up one of the pocket testaments we provide to everyone who does not have a Bible.

Later that evening, the young woman with the tear in her eye following Communion was killed in a tragic car accident. Only hours earlier, as a stranger, she had been welcomed at our church. Someone like you welcomed her at the door. Someone like you greeted her in worship. Someone like you looked her in the eye, gave her a piece of the bread, shared the cup, and offered her Christ. Someone like you handed her a Bible for the first time. Someone like you bore witness to her of the love of the One who came to seek and save those who are lost, of the One who redeems us, and of the One in whom we know that death does not have the final answer.

The ministry of notice has life-transforming impact. How will you notice and welcome others with Christ's love?

Let us pray: *Jesus, you noticed people. You heard the cry of the blind man, you noticed the woman who touched the hem of your robe, you noticed children. Help me see people as you see them. Help me have a curiosity about others around me. Help me not to become so distracted by the task or so busy that I don't see others around me. Lord, I lay aside my own desires, needs, and wants so that I might be used by you in ministry in my community and in the world. Help me find ways to be your hands and feet, to begin practicing hospitality in all aspects of my life so that it flows naturally in all that I do, bearing witness to my love for you. Amen.*

Personal Reflection

1. Describe a time when you felt unnoticed. What were you feeling?

2. In Romans 12:13 we read, "When God's people are in need, be ready to help them. Always be eager to practice hospitality" (NLT). Where can you practice the ministry of notice with greater intentionality and commitment at church? at work? at home?

3. What reliable systems are needed in your church to capture names, ensure timely follow-up, and make certain the environment is prepared for guests? What can you personally do to support these systems and set a positive example?

4. Share a time when you have either said or heard someone say, "I was in the right place at the right time." Describe the circumstances and where you see the ministry of notice in that situation.

5. When do you find yourself too busy to notice? Where do you need to slow down?

6. **Where do you find discouragement, biases, and judgments as barriers to the ministry of notice?**

7. **When you consider the impact of the ministry of notice, what is one action step you will take?**

3

THE THREE QUESTIONS

When it comes to extending exceptional hospitality, we won't get far unless we understand why it's important—what the good news means to us and why we are called to share it with others. Taking biblical hospitality seriously, sacrificing our own comfort and preferences to make others comfortable, is likely to mean changes both in our church and in our individual lives. But if we understand why we are called to do these things, we can stay focused and committed even when the change becomes difficult. Understanding why we do the things we do is vitally important as we strive to live out our purpose.

As Christians, biblical hospitality is our natural response to the good news of Jesus Christ in our lives. It flows from our compelling mission to share this good news with others. But what precisely is the good news? What is the message we are called to share?

The good news is nothing less than the unconditional love and salvation we have received in Jesus, which Jesus offers to the whole world. There are many ways to sum up this message of good news, but my favorite is the summary offered by Karl Barth, one of the greatest theologians of the twentieth century. Barth wrote many volumes—thousands of pages, millions of words—to explore and explain Christian theology. Yet when someone asked him to summarize the essence of what he believed, he simply quoted the well-known hymn often taught to children: "Jesus loves me this I know, for the Bible tells me so."

The good news is indescribably deep, but at its heart it is simple enough for all people to grasp. As those called to be messengers of this good news, we also need a simple way of explaining what we believe and why it matters. This can help us understand our own purpose and how exceptional hospitality fits into it, and it will also help us share the good news with others and take the all-important step of inviting those outside the church to come and see.

Three questions are especially helpful to guide us in understanding the good news and why it matters to others. Reflecting on these three questions is essential to our authenticity as individuals and as a church as we turn our attention outward.

1. Why do people need Jesus Christ?
2. Why do people need the church?
3. Why do people need your church?

Why Do People Need Jesus Christ?

The first question we must be able to answer is, "Why do people need Jesus Christ?" Not why would Jesus Christ be a nice thing for people to have in their lives—why do people *need* him? As a church, you are called to make disciples of Jesus Christ, inviting people to follow him. You aren't inviting them to join a club or show up to an event once a week. You are inviting them to change their lives and commit or surrender to Jesus Christ. So why should they do it? Why do people need Jesus Christ?

Living in a pluralistic world, we are sometimes not really clear about that anymore. Yet it's vital for you as an individual and for your church to recognize what Jesus means to you and what he could mean for others. It's worthwhile for you to pause, reflect, and maybe even wrestle with why you believe.

In *Leading Beyond the Walls*, Adam Hamilton writes,

> Now, here's the conviction that I came to be seized by: Jesus Christ is the solution to the deepest longings of the human heart. He is the answer to the most serious problems that plague our society. When Jesus is Lord and the Holy Spirit enters the heart of the believer, we find…the process of becoming "new creatures in Christ."…
>
> Why do people need Christ? Because without him we will always be lost and our lives will never realize their God-given potential. He opens the door to a whole new world for us. He enriches every life he touches. He changes the world one person at a time, as his kingdom expands across the globe.[1]

At Resurrection, we are convinced that people need Jesus Christ because he alone satisfies the deepest longings of the human heart. People will not find their deepest needs met by buying the newest technology gadget or in another person. The need for unconditional grace and mercy, the need to believe that there's hope for the future, the need to know that in the darkest moments of our lives the darkness will not prevail—we can't find anywhere else but in Jesus Christ. Jesus Christ, who says in John 11:25, "I am the resurrection and the life. Whoever believes in me will live, even though they die," provides hope when we have been diagnosed with a terminal illness. When we are struggling with relationships and marriage, we can find no other hope than in the One who can change hearts. The problems in our world from racism, discrimination, polarization, poverty, and war, at their core, are all spiritual problems and have to do with the human condition that is broken in us which can only be addressed by Jesus Christ.

We must be absolutely convinced of this—that Jesus Christ is good news and the only true hope for the world—if we are going to reach people for him and be willing to make the sacrifices necessary to do so. It must be something we personally believe so strongly that when we share our conviction with others, they can see it in our eyes and hear it in our tone of voice. We must fundamentally believe that Jesus Christ is essential for being fully human. He is the answer to the deepest longings of our soul. We must believe that our faith in Jesus has made a difference in our lives.

We must not only believe but also be able to communicate it to others in a way that they can receive it. We must have an answer to this question: "Why do people need Jesus?" That answer must resonate with people who are unconvinced of their need for Jesus Christ. It must be compelling to them, not just to us. I've found that the best way to do this is by sharing my faith story. People respond to personal stories far more readily than arguments or information. The best way to share the good news of Jesus Christ is to share the authentic story of what Jesus has done in your life.

What is your story? Here is mine. I grew up in a Christian home, exposed to church and Sunday school every weekend. And while I had experienced the transforming presence of Christ in my life through my baptism and confirmation, I would not fully realize it until later in my twenties. I had married an amazing but nonreligious man, and church attendance became an easily forgotten practice. Several years into our marriage, with children, demanding careers, and a stressed relationship, my husband agreed to give this "church thing" a try in an effort to save our marriage. Through the welcome of our church community, we experienced the transforming love of Christ. We discovered sacrificial love, as demonstrated by Christ when he gave up his life for us so that we might find life. The message of the Gospels became alive to us. We both fell in love with Jesus, who loves us unconditionally and called us to love one another unconditionally. This unconditional love has saved our marriage time and time again over the past three decades.

We discovered a God who, through his son Jesus, demonstrated his love and compassion for those who were far from faith, those who were marginalized, hurting, outcast, ordinary sinners, and prodigals like me. We experienced a God who loves, forgives, and longs to draw his children to himself. And as we fell more and more in love with Jesus, this love compelled us as his followers to share it with others, to love our neighbors and to do unto others as we would have them do to us. Our lives have been transformed, the lives of our family have been transformed, and while we don't get it perfect, continuing to stumble and make mistakes, we strive to live for Christ each day.

I am a better wife, mother, grandmother, daughter, friend, aunt, and staff member because of what Christ has done in my life. While I may not be fully able to explain all the difference he has made in my life, I know my life is better because of my decision to follow Jesus.

What is your story? Why do you need Jesus? What difference has Jesus made in your life? We have the greatest story in the history of eternity to share, if only we could remember it.

A recent study by the Pew Research Center shows that "more than eight-in-ten members of the Silent Generation...describe themselves as Christians (84%), as do three-quarters of Baby Boomers (76%). In stark contrast, only half of Millennials (49%) describe themselves as Christians."[2] The study goes on to describe Millennials and subsequent generations as having a declining interest in religion, meaning that the trend is downward. It seems that people in our society are increasingly viewing church as irrelevant.

Church, we must find a way to share the message of the good news with those who have yet to hear it *in a way to which they can relate and respond.* For too long we have not been willing to change and now find ourselves looking at communities that have changed all around us. We are not called to change the message of the good news, but we must find new, authentic ways to share it with new generations of people who have not heard it or experienced it or who view it as irrelevant in their lives.

Your story is what they need. You may not have an expertly crafted, theologically astute explanation, but you do have a story to share. When the blind man was healed in John 9:25, he didn't have a deep theological response to who Jesus was, but he was able to respond with what he had personally experienced: "I don't know whether he's a sinner. Here's what I do know: I was blind and now I see." People come to Christ largely because other people had the courage, with gentleness and respect, to bear witness to their faith.

And so it begins with you. Why do people need Jesus? What is your story? What do others see as a witness to the difference Christ has made in your life? While I don't always get it right, my desire is that someone might be drawn to meet Christ because of something they have seen in me.

Why Do People Need the Church?

The second question we must ask is, "Why do people need the church?" It is important to remember that you are inviting people not only to follow Jesus but also to become a part of the church. We just read in the previous pages that there are many who don't believe they need Christ, and if they don't need Christ, they surely don't need the church. There are others who might be willing to give Jesus a try, but remain distrustful of organized religion. Some believe the church is narrow-minded and composed of hypocrites. Some believe all we want is their money. Others feel the church is irrelevant, out of touch, and boring.

So if people are not convinced they need organized religion, how do you persuade them they need the church? Why do *you* need the church?

We may have come to misunderstand the church as a building, or a place where we go to attend a worship service, a funeral, or a wedding. But the biblical church is not a building or place. Buildings are important tools and provide the physical spaces that churches inhabit and use for worship and fellowship, Christian discipleship, and mission. But the church is really an assembly or group of people.

The New Testament makes it clear that the church is not our idea. The church was Jesus's idea. He said of Peter, "I'll build my church on this rock. The gates of the underworld won't be able to stand against it" (Matthew 16:18). "*My* church" (emphasis added), Jesus says. Jesus is the one who builds it. The disciples were the beginning of a new movement inviting others to join in a body that has a unique relationship to God through Jesus Christ.

When Jesus refers to the church, he is not speaking of a building or specific denomination, but rather to all people who follow him. He is the head of the church, as we read in Colossians 1:18: "He is the head of the body, the church, who is the beginning, the one who is firstborn from among the dead so that he might occupy the first place in everything." Jesus established his church with Peter and the other disciples and invites us to participate in building and continuing the church today. We are called to this fellowship, this assembly, this church to care for one another, encourage one another, and work together for good. And we are not meant to do it alone. We are meant to do it within the community, the assembly, the church.

Acts 2:42-47 gives us a glimpse of what it means to be the church. We see an assembly of people overwhelmed by the love of Jesus and gathered together for worship, study, prayer, fellowship, and shared meals. They also gave of their resources to help others in need:

> The believers devoted themselves to the apostles' teaching, to the community, to their shared meals, and to their prayers. A sense of awe came over everyone. God performed many wonders and signs through the

apostles. All the believers were united and shared everything. They would sell pieces of property and possessions and distribute the proceeds to everyone who needed them. Every day, they met together in the temple and ate in their homes. They shared food with gladness and simplicity. They praised God and demonstrated God's goodness to everyone. The Lord added daily to the community those who were being saved.

I am convinced that we can never be the kind of Christian God wants us to be without other Christians. We need each other. It is in the context of relationships that our lives are transformed. It is through community that we are inspired, challenged, and held accountable, all of which is difficult to do on our own. Why do people need the church? Because people need Jesus and none of us can follow Jesus on our own. We need the companionship and support of others who are following Jesus too.

At my church, we hear stories weekly of how lives are being changed at Resurrection through worship, small groups, and missions. There is something powerful that happens when we gather each weekend as a community of faith to hear the word spoken, to sing songs of praise, to offer our prayers together, to share our gifts and offerings, and to participate in Holy Communion. There is something powerful that happens when we gather to study scripture together in small groups. Something powerful happens when you realize that you don't have to do this alone. We experience the presence of the Holy Spirit in extraordinary ways when we are together in community. Through community, we also have the opportunity to serve others. God gave each of us different spiritual gifts, and we need one another's gifts.

As a church community, we pray for one another and we care for another. Right after joining Resurrection, my husband was still trying to be a weekend flag football warrior and suffered a full Achilles tendon tear while in a tournament out of state. Once back in Kansas City, we went directly to the hospital for immediate surgery. When we arrived at the hospital, we were met by a small group of people from the church, whom we had only barely met, waiting to pray with us before Reed went into surgery. They sat with me in the waiting room during the surgery and continued to visit throughout the time Reed remained in the hospital. For the following month, meals arrived at our home. These meals were such a welcome blessing as I cared for our two toddlers and my husband as he healed and while I maintained my work outside our home. These acts of kindness from our church gave me such comfort and peace during a time when I was feeling afraid and alone. To this day I have never forgotten the blessing of having a church community.

Together as a community, we can accomplish for God more than any of us can accomplish by ourselves. It is amazing to me to see what a group of people committed to the same goals can do. When we put our resources of time and money together, we can impact change in our communities and world. My husband and I led a disaster recovery response trip to Puerto Rico. Our mission team of twelve people was able to prep and paint the outside of a local church that had been destroyed in Hurricane Maria; put down tile in a house for a woman who had lost her entire home; and replace cabinets in the home of an elderly woman in the community. We accomplished all of this in five days, working together in a way that none of us alone could have accomplished. This is just one example of the power of the church working together.

There is a difference between coming to church and being the church. Occasionally, some may say,

"I don't need the church." But as followers of Jesus, it's not just that you need the church—the church needs you! There are people who need you to show up, to offer a word of encouragement, to lead a class, to be a greeter, to extend welcome. The church wasn't intended to be an audience of people coming for a performance and leaving after the service is over. The church is a community of people caring for one another! Instead of looking at the church as a place where you can have your needs met, you begin to view it as a place where you can be used by God to meet the needs of others. You help them experience belonging, community, acceptance, and support. When you take this seriously, it means you are looking around to see who is alone, who may need a friend, who needs encouragement. It is inviting people to sit by you or asking if you can sit by them. It is checking on and caring for others. This is part of our responsibility as the church.

We are called to be a communion of saints. That doesn't mean we are perfect, but that we are seeking to give ourselves to Christ, yield our lives to him, and to do his work in the world together, living lives defined by love.

So what is the church? It's the body of Christ, doing what Christ would be doing if he were here physically on earth. Why do people need the church? People need the church because following Jesus was never meant to be a solo journey. We need one another. The church is a community that celebrates with us, grieves with us, lifts us up, gives us hope, challenges us to grow, and helps us be the best version of ourselves that we can possibly be. The church is the way Jesus joins his followers together as family, as a community. You need others, and others need you.

The church is the continuing presence of Christ in the world. Jesus came two thousand years ago to show us the way and has called us through the power of the Holy Spirit to be his continuing presence, to continue his saving work in the world as the church.

Why Do People Need Your Church?

Now that you've reflected on why people need Jesus and why people need the church, it's time to get more specific. The third question is, "Why do people need *your* church?" Why should someone follow Jesus within your community rather than in a different community of believers?

This was a very important question for us. When Church of the Resurrection was starting, there were dozens of other churches starting at about the same time. So, why start another church? Recognizing that the other churches were also offering valid expressions of faith, we needed to be clear about our distinctives as a congregation. What is it that we offer that might reach someone that the other churches might not reach? We needed to be clear about what was special about our particular congregation. Not what made us better than others, but what was special about us. What would we be known for in the community?

At Resurrection we have identified four distinctives that define our congregation. They are our answer to why people need our church. The first distinctive is that we are *outwardly focused*. We strive to reach people who are not connected to a church or to God, and we strive to serve the community and the world, particularly those most vulnerable. Our second distinctive is to be *thought-provoking*. Our aim is to engage people in critical thinking, encouraging people to ask questions and engage their intellect while also engaging their heart. One way we do this is through preaching sermons that are aimed at reaching thinking people. We are not afraid to tackle controversial issues while looking to scripture for context and to see what Jesus said and did. Our third distinctive is be *bridge-building*. We are a church that seeks to build bridges across the theological, political, and sociological divide. We are welcoming, not judging, and we strive for a community in which individuals with different socioeconomic statuses, political views, skin colors, and sexual orientations sit next to one another each weekend and serve together in the community, committed to a common purpose and vision as a church. Our fourth distinctive is to be *hope-radiating*. Our hope is rooted in the resurrection of Christ, and this is captured in the name of our church. We believe there is always hope and seek to give hope through an unshakable faith rooted in Jesus Christ to people walking through dark or uncertain times.

These may not be the distinctives of your church. Yours may be different, but knowing what is unique and special about your church is important whether you are a new church or an established, century-old congregation. And it starts with being clear on your purpose. Growing churches that practice biblical hospitality are clear on their purpose and resolutely set out to work with God to accomplish that purpose.

Do you have a clear understanding of your church's purpose? Can you answer the question, "Why my church?" Is the purpose connected to your congregation's calling, a knowledge of the community around you and the needs of the people, and an understanding of what might be required to reach them?

At Resurrection, we know not only our distinctives but also why our church exists. Our purpose is clearly understood by everyone in our congregation, and it defines everything we do. Our purpose is *to build a Christian community where nonreligious and nominally religious people are becoming deeply committed Christians.* Every person in leadership, and we hope, most of our members, can recite this purpose statement from memory. Our purpose statement is written in large letters in our lobbies so that all who enter or leave our buildings are reminded of why we exist. During planning meetings where we design sermon series, worship elements, new programs, brochures and flyers, and fellowship events, and in committee meetings where we make decisions about finances, infrastructure, buildings, and other matters, we constantly ask ourselves: "If we make this decision, how will it help a nonreligious or nominally religious person become a deeply committed Christian? How will it help us be outwardly focused, thought-provoking, bridge-building, or hope-radiating?" If we don't have a compelling answer, we don't move forward. Our purpose statement and distinctives guide all we do.

So how did we get clarity of purpose? We invested time in answering the three questions, "Why do people need Jesus? Why do people need the church? Why do people need our church?" We prayed. We studied scripture. We studied our community. We sought God's guidance.

Jesus said,

> You are the light of the world. A city on top of a hill can't be hidden. Neither do people light a lamp and put it under a basket. Instead, they put it on top of a lampstand, and it shines on all who are in the house. In the same way, let your light shine before people, so they can see the good things you do and praise your Father who is in heaven.
>
> (Matthew 5:14-16)

The "you" Jesus mentions here is plural—you, together as the church, are the light of the world. We each have a little light we're meant to let shine, and when we let our lights shine together, we can really make a difference. What is your light as a church? What are you known for in the community? What do civic leaders, school leaders, nonprofits, and business owners know your church for? What about the server in the local café, or students in the community? What do they say about your church?

Take a moment and consider why someone might want to attend your church. Write down four things they would find at your church to be compelling to them.

Now, if it was hard for you to name four reasons, you will want to spend time as a church discussing the opportunities that exist to reach new people, new "neighbors" in your area, and what changes may need to happen to reach them. Take time together brainstorming ideas, identifying opportunities and your strengths as a congregation. Talk to other groups who are doing this study, or to your pastor who is supporting this vision of radical hospitality. What can your church do or be for others that no other church can? Why do people need your church?

During a consultation with a local church who was making plans for a building renovation, I asked them to share why they were undertaking this renovation and to name their objectives. "Well," one said, "we want to grow the church. We want to see our membership increase. We need younger people."

I pressed the leaders, asking how this renovation might actually help them reach younger people. I asked, "What are you inviting them to? What will they experience? Why should they come to your church? Is worship excellent? Is there a small group for them? Do you have a nursery for their children?" The conversation went silent. The church realized there was a lot of work to do and that the renovation was not the sole answer.

The answer you might provide as to why someone should attend your church cannot be driven by the need to increase membership or to keep your doors open. Your objective must be on reaching individuals wherever they are, however they are, building a relationship with your neighbors to share the good news of Jesus Christ and meeting their needs. It must be a biblical hospitality that constantly looks and reaches outward. You and your fellow church members should be inviting others easily and without hesitation because you know what good your church does and why someone should come.

Several years ago, a woman visited our church and after several additional visits decided to join.

She had just moved to our area and shared that a neighbor had told her about our church. When asked the neighbor's name, she replied that we would not know the neighbor because the neighbor did not go to our church. He told her about our church, saying, "You won't like my church. But I've heard good things about this church called Church of the Resurrection. You should visit there."

Obviously, you don't want to say that about your church. You want to be able to say, "Oh, this is where I go to church, and I love it! Here are the things I love, and here is why you should come with me!"

Friends, this is very important. Whatever your role at church, you must believe in your church and help everyone else in your congregation believe in it too. Boost your fellow members' self-esteem. Give language to articulate why it is such a great blessing to be counted as a member of your church. Name and claim the amazing work that God is doing and will do in your church.

Most parents can relate to the importance of helping children have self-esteem. My husband and I made it a priority to find ways to help our children believe in themselves and see their potential. When our son was in fourth grade, his curriculum required ten minutes of daily writing in a journal. In one journal entry he wrote, "I love my dad because even when I don't think I am good at hitting the baseball, he tells me I am doing a good job and he is proud of me. This gives me confidence when I am up at the plate and helps me believe in myself." Our son didn't make it to the major leagues, but he did play four years of college baseball. The ways in which my husband intentionally shaped our son's self-esteem helped our son see his potential. In this same way, you need to help shape your church's self-esteem and enable those around you to see its potential. And you don't have to be a church leader to do this. Whoever you are, whatever your role, you can recognize what God is doing and can do among you and speak up, helping others to see it too.

What is the potential of your church and its ministries to your community? In what ways are you helping your church see that it is remarkable? Are you proud and excited to be serving in your church and to tell others about it? When a church begins to believe in itself, amazing things can happen.

I was inspired by a church in a rural area who spent time seeking God's direction for their church. The congregation was aging and attendance was declining. As a church body, they asked what they were each really great at doing. In a God moment, they recognized that they were each really great at being grandparents. So, they decided their distinctive was to be "grandparents to the community." They named the roles of grandparents and began fulfilling similar roles by volunteering in the local school, preparing meals for families with newborns, babysitting, and opening up the church for after-school programs and summer camps. This built a bridge to their community, and it is what they are known for now among the people around them. They carry biblical hospitality beyond their doors because they recognized why their church existed and how it could be a blessing to others.

So why your church? Churches are imperfect but chosen organizations on a mission given by Christ. Your church is God's chosen instrument to bear the light of hope to your community. It is a daily mission to see what is broken, who is broken, where the world is messed up, or where there is pain, indifference, or injustice, and do something about it. Imagine the difference in your community if each person in your congregation, empowered by the Holy Spirit, daily sought to embody the message of Jesus.

Listen to how Peter describes the church in 1 Peter 2:9: "But you are a chosen race, a royal priesthood, a holy nation, a people who are God's own possession. You have become this people so that you may speak of the wonderful acts of the one who called you out of darkness into his amazing light." Church, you are chosen to be the body of Christ. Together we must incarnate God's love and Christ's presence. It is by your relentless focus on your purpose and your distinct acts of mercy, compassion, and service that people will be drawn to Christ and drawn to your church.

Let us pray: *God, through your son, Jesus Christ, we desire to be your church. We recognize that first we must individually yield our lives to be transformed by your love, so we give our lives to you. Give us a bold vision for the ministry and mission you have called us to do as a church, and give us the passion to pursue it. Help us to see others as you see them. Make us instruments of your peace, mercy, justice, and welcome to all in our community. Amen.*

Personal Reflection

1. Why do you need Jesus Christ? Think about your story. Make notes in a journal. Consider your life before Christ. What has Jesus done in your life? What does your life look like now as you walk with him? What difference has Jesus made in your life?

2. How would you respond to a nonreligious person about why they need Jesus Christ?

3. If someone were to ask you "What is the church?" how would you answer? When have you seen the church in action and been amazed at how God brings us all together?

4. We all carry a lifetime of experiences and perspectives. On a piece of paper, make two columns. In one column list the negative adjectives you have either experienced or heard others use to describe the church. In the second column, list positive adjectives. Share together as a group. Keep this list visible in your Bible or another place where you

can see it. What will you personally do
to help your church live into the positive
adjectives you listed?

5. As you begin to look at what it means
to be the church, write down hopes,
assumptions, and dreams you have for
the church. Take a moment to share them
with the group.

6. What is the purpose of your church?
What is unique about your church?
Of all the churches in the area, why
should someone choose yours?

7. Why does knowing the answers to the
three questions posed in this chapter
help us see the importance of radical
hospitality?

8. Thinking of your answers to the
questions of why people need Jesus, why
they need the church, and why they need
your church, what is one action step
that you can take right away to extend
hospitality to others in your community?

NOTES

1. BIBLICAL HOSPITALITY

1. Jill Bremer, "Seven Minutes and Counting," in *Fusion: Turning First-Time Guests into Fully-Engaged Members of Your Church*, eds. Nelson Searcy and Jennifer Dykes Henson (Grand Rapids: Baker, 2007), 49; Tyler Schmall, "This Is Exactly How Long You Have to Make a Good First Impression," *New York Post,* December 14, 2018, https://nypost.com/2018/12/14/this-is-exactly-how-long -you-have-to-make-a-good-first-impression/.

2. Robert Schnase, *Five Practices of Fruitful Congregations* (Nashville: Abingdon Press, 2007), 21, 20.

3. THE THREE QUESTIONS

1. Adam Hamilton, *Leading Beyond the Walls* (Nashville: Abingdon Press, 2002), 22-23.

2. "In U.S., Decline of Christianity Continues at Rapid Pace," Pew Research Center, October 17, 2019, www.pewforum .org/2019/10/17/in-u-s-decline-of-christianity-continues-at -rapid-pace/.